Talking through Pictures

A Beginner's Guide to Photojournalism

by Jürg Wittwer
with Jessica Holom

For Cornelia

ISBN: 1523232021

ISBN-13: 978-1523232024

Contents

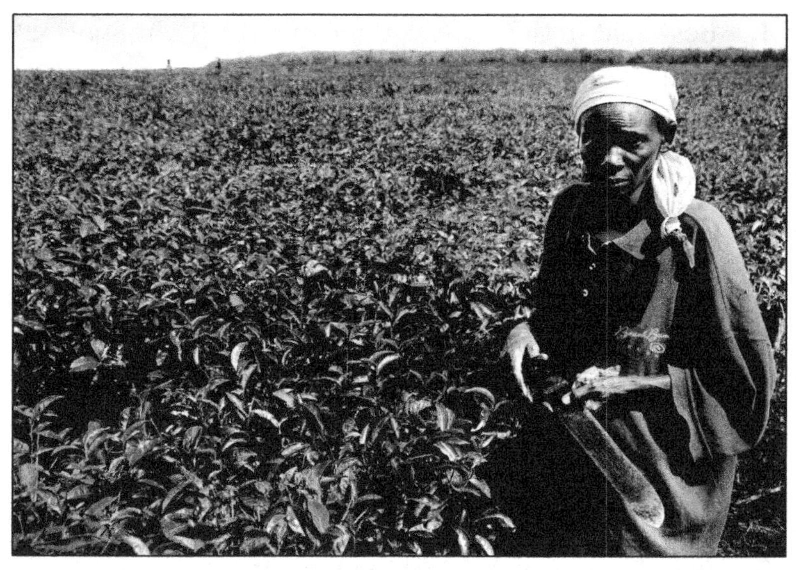

Foreword

We are consumers. Every day, we consume food, drink, products, and we even consume pictures. Lots of pictures. We see them in newspapers, magazines, digital print and, as consumers, we don't think twice about what we consume. So let's think twice: after you weed out the garbage, the meat of what we consume is art; art in the form of photojournalism. This art has been around since the dawn of photography. But technology has evolved. Colored photos have replaced black-and-white ones. With the digital revolution, film rolls and the dark room have evaporated. But throughout this evolution of photography, the job of the photojournalist has remained the same: to capture a moment in time, to tell a story without words. This book will provide you short tips and simple tools to make pictures like a pro. In reading this book, I sincerely hope you enjoy, learn, and grow as a photographer. Moreover, my goal in writing about and sharing my experience is to improve your work's potential for publication.

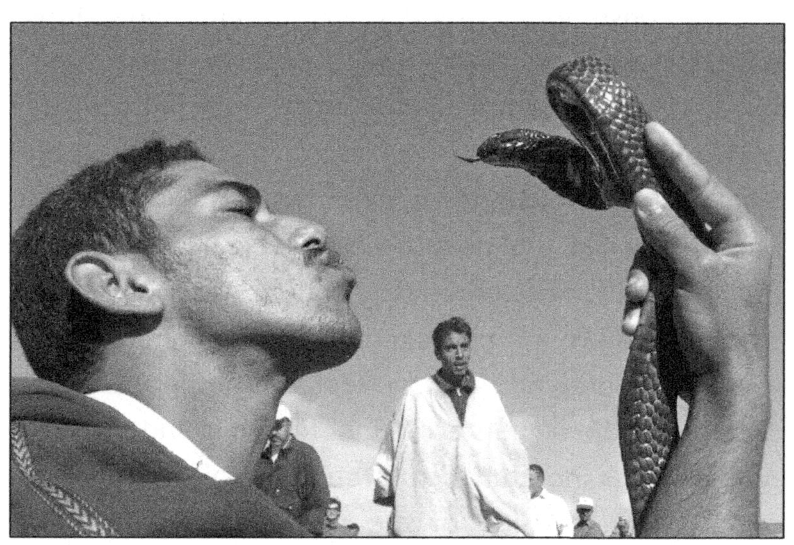

1. Best Seat in the House: Choosing the Right Spot

The most important decision you'll make when it comes to taking an excellent photo has nothing to do with your camera or your lens. Composition is key to visual appeal, so your foremost task is to choose the right spot from which to shoot.

Think of it this way: when you book a ticket to a movie or a football game, you choose the best seat available in order to have the optimal view. The same idea applies to photography. To take the best picture, you must choose the best seat in the venue – in other words, choose the "right" spot.

The position where you stand defines the composition of your photograph. Imagine an empty parking lot. A tree grows in the middle of the lot and, in front of the tree, stands your model. The perspective and layout of the composition *you* create for this scene, however, depends on where you position your camera. The tree will be to the right of the model in your photo when you take your shot from the left. If you shoot from behind the tree, the tree will be either partially or entirely in front of the model, blocking him or her from view. When you are positioned dead-center, the tree will be growing from your model's head and, if the camera is zoomed in for a close-up, you can eliminate the tree from the composition altogether. The point is, if you don't walk around and experiment with the positioning of your camera, then you're bound to miss the perfect shot. In any case, not bothering to consider various angles and perspectives means you're not placing enough emphasis on the composition of your picture.

If you ask a studio photographer to name the most important aspect of photography, he or she will probably emphasize the value of lighting. A photojournalist, on the other hand, does not have the luxury to freely arrange studio flashes, nor can he/she place the models on their "marks" to ensure they catch the best light. Photojournalism is so engaging because it captures the spontaneity of a moment in time in all of its natural beauty. The only thing you have full control over as a photographer is your position. In choosing the right spot, you decide where the available light comes from, where the subject appears, and how the background is arranged in the picture. Whereas light may be the most important aspect of studio photography, your own perspective and intuition - in other words, choosing the right spot from which to shoot - will be what tells the story you want to tell.

If you want to photograph in a way that no one else has, to produce a composition that has yet to be produced, then you must stand where no one else stands or has stood. Before you take your shot, look around, walk around, and choose your unique position.

For most occasions, the best spots are limited. If you've attended any highly publicized event, you will have noticed that all journalists and photographers are jockeying for the same position, throwing elbows and getting in each other's way. This is because the ideal composition is often universal. Man's visual perception of "beauty" when it comes to the layout of a photograph or of a painting is surprisingly standard the world over. This is why the composition of Van Gogh's "Starry Night," for instance, appeals to many; because, to a certain degree, our eyes work to gauge beauty in the same way. Sure, beauty is "in the eye of the beholder," but this does not necessarily mean that no universal ideal exists. That being said, your composition does not have to be this ideal in order to be considered visually intriguing; it can be new and unique and still appeal to the masses.

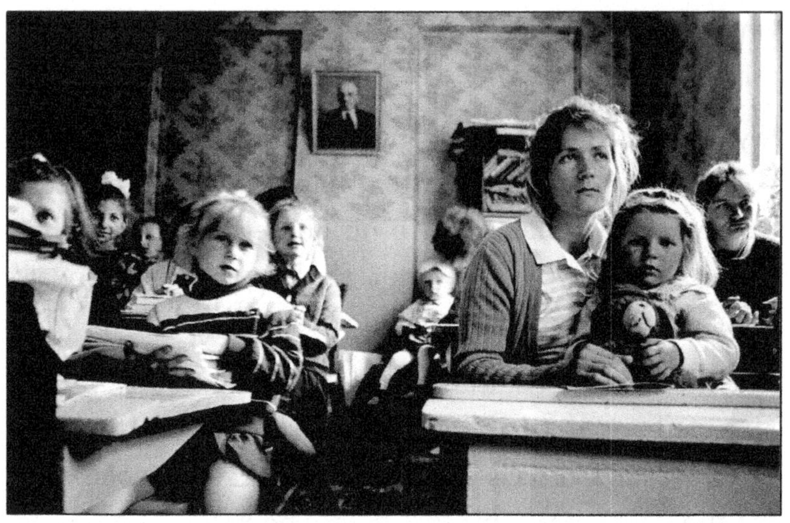

This picture was taken in a room with little space. I was forced to kneel down in front of the teacher's desk and use a wide-angle lens. The position allowed me to be at the height of the children's eyes and at the feet of Lenin's portrait at the far end of the room. The position in front of the gangway separating two rows of desks also allowed me to fit many children into the frame, who would normally have been hidden by the front row. Do not be afraid to kneel, crouch down, or even lie down to find your ideal position and perspective.

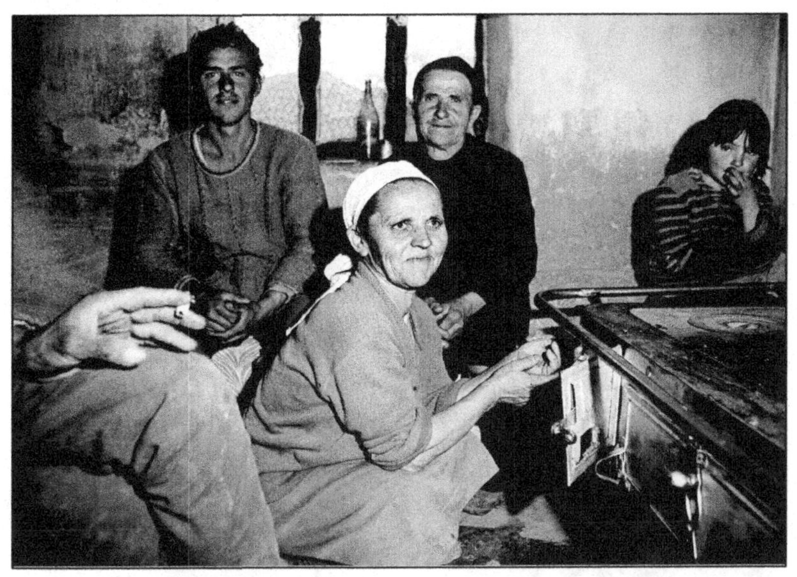

Set in the Albanian mountains shortly after the fall of the dictator Enver Hoxha, again I knelt on the floor to be at the same height as the women. It allowed me to include the hand with cigarette, while emphasizing the endearing semicircle of a close-knit family warming themselves by the stove.

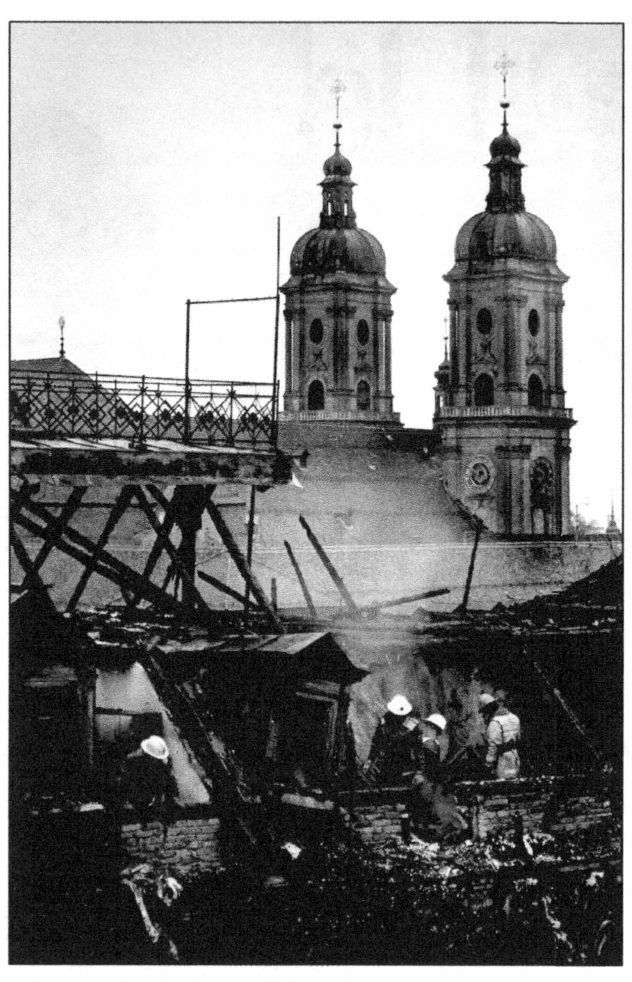

In the early nineties, a fire destroyed four houses in the old town of St. Gallen. The best spot from which to photograph the destruction was the women's toilet on the top floor of a five-star hotel. Inevitably, one after another, the town's photojournalists filed in to take their pictures.

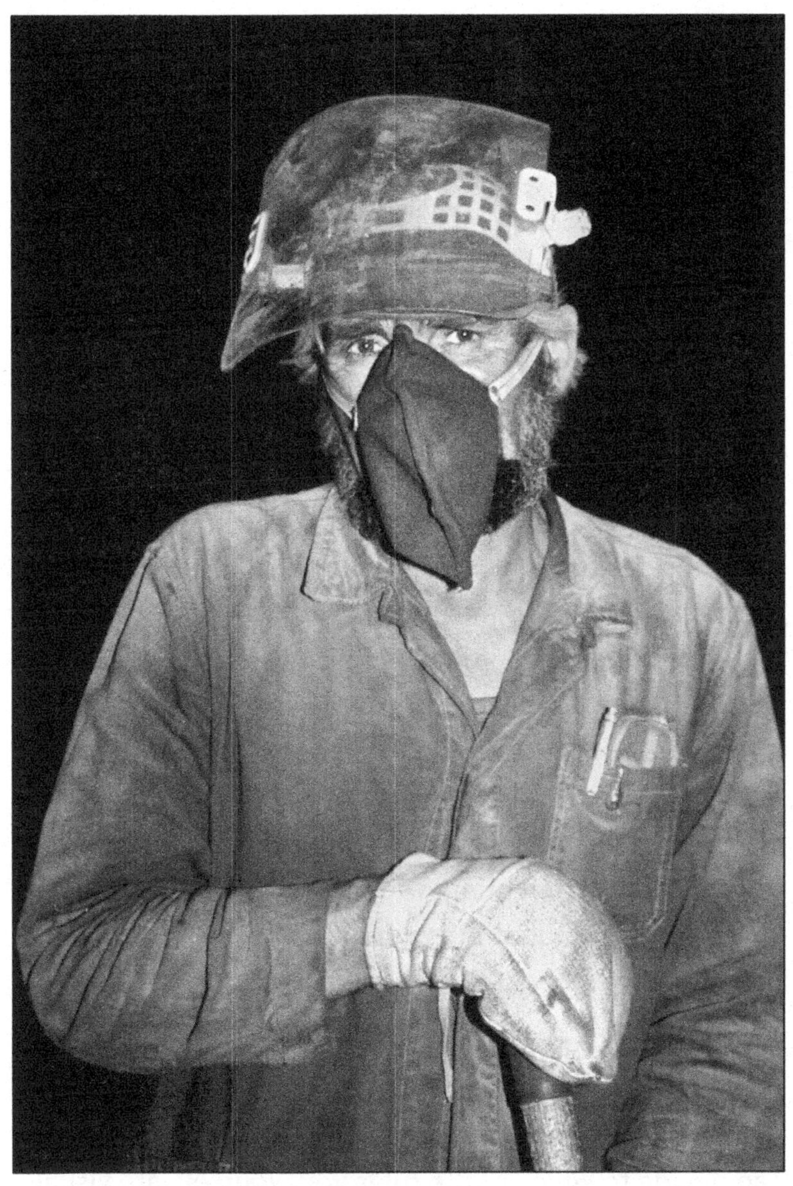

2. Strike Some Intrigue: Using Compositional Elements

In choosing the right spot, you define the perspective, the background, and the objects you wish to frame in the picture. To arrange them in order that they possess striking visual impact, a timeless set of compositional rules exist, one with which you should make yourself familiar. Whether you're an amateur photographer just starting out or an advanced photographer who needs a refresher, experimenting with compositional rules will always endow your photos with time-tested truths when it comes to aesthetics.

This book will quickly cover three of these useful compositional rules. As your skillset grows, you will experiment with increasingly complex compositions, and you can decide to which of the rules you, yourself, are visually attracted. Our personal visual perception defines certain aspects as aesthetic or beautiful, but as stated in chapter 1, an objective universal idea of beauty and ideal aesthetics does come into play. These principles have been remarkably constant over time, which tells us something about humanity: our taste is consistent when it comes to proportion and composition. The painters of the 15th and 16th century used the same basic compositional tactics, as you may use in your photography today.

Golden Ratio

The Golden Ratio goes back even further than the Renaissance. The ancient Greeks studied this ratio, because it appeared often in geometry and in nature, so often that they were fascinated by it. The Parthenon's façade is littered with golden rectangles, and the proportions of many Greek statues, dating back to 400 BC, embody the Golden Ratio as well. But what is this ratio and how can you apply it to photography?

Let's imagine we want to capture the endlessness of the sea in a picture. The day is a nice one for photography, with a glorious cloud and sun constellation in the sky. As an amateur photographer, your first reflex might be to line up the horizon across the middle, dividing the picture evenly between sky and sea. But what happens if you do not divide evenly, if you show more sea or more sky, moving the horizon up or down just a tad? When you do this, the picture becomes more dynamic. If you play a little with framing the horizon, you will land on a spot where the picture feels perfect. Chances are this perfect position will place your horizon spot-on the Golden Ratio. That sweet spot lies around 4/10 from either the top or the bottom of the image, as well as from the left and right. When taking pictures, you're not about to pull out a ruler and calculator to measure and compute figures, so simply eyeball the ratio by about a third, and then correct slightly according to feeling.

In the picture on the next page, this boy from Mozambique is carrying tobacco leaves. His head lies close to the Golden Ratio of the rectangular frame, vertically and horizontally. Using the right hand horizontal, the weight of the picture is tilted towards the direction the boy is walking, emphasizing his movement.

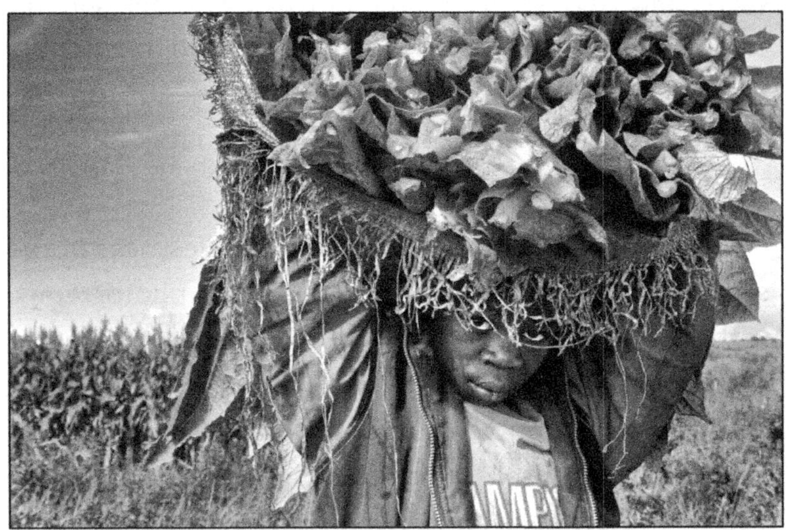

Symmetry

The concept of symmetry applies not only to visual art, but to math and the sciences and can be defined in a number of ways. For the purpose of photography, intuition plays a key role in defining symmetry. As we look in our camera lens, we may line up an image so that two sides of an object or a picture look the same. This is symmetry. Visually, the power of symmetry does not lie in whether this mirroring is horizontal, vertical or diagonal. Nor does the symmetry need to be an exact mirror image in order to pull off the desired effect. For instance, more often than not, fashion models have generally symmetrical faces – as this is what we consider ideal or beautiful – , but still the two halves of the faces differ. In photography, if the eye recognizes symmetry, this is sufficient in the creation of a compelling photograph. Exactitude and precision is unnecessary. An example of symmetry in a typical landscape photograph is the reflection of a tree in the water. A tree alongside a river would be rather boring on its own. With the addition of a symmetrical reflection, the photo becomes exponentially more intriguing.

You can also use symmetry to frame a picture. For instance, to place your model or focal point between two similar houses, identical windows, or trees, you create an interesting dynamic and draw the viewer's attention to that person or focal point. There are unlimited possibilities when it comes to using symmetry in composition.

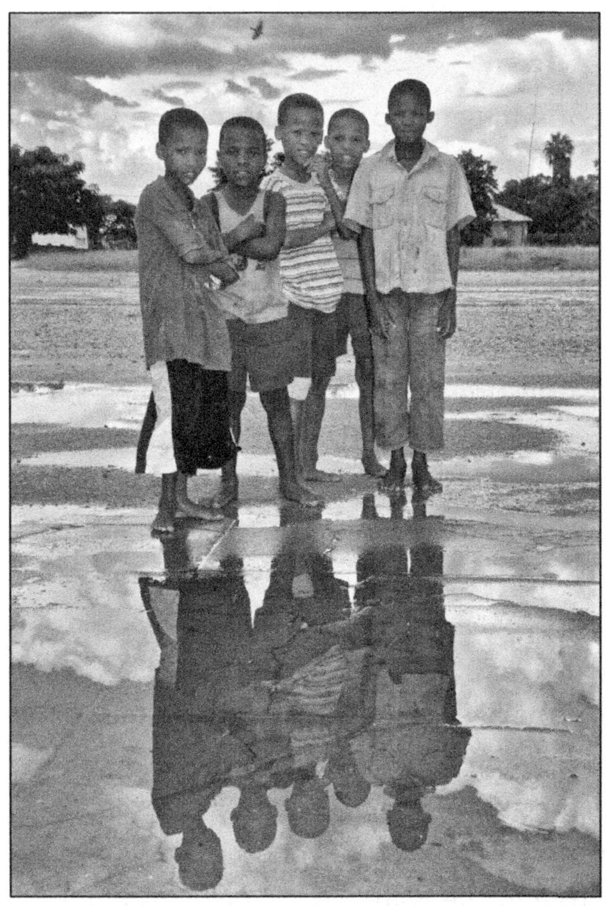

The human eye reacts strongly to symmetry in all forms. And this is what you want as a photographer – a strong reaction from your audience – because this indicates that you've communicated your story.

The picture above was taken in Namibia. The photo's visual strength is driven by the symmetrical reflection of the boys in the water.

Diagonals

In geometry, a diagonal is a line between two non-consecutive angles of an object. In photography, your diagonal is an imaginary line across the picture from a lower corner to the opposite upper corner. Using diagonals to drive your photo's visual dynamics can result in incredible dramatic effects. The diagonal guides the eye across the entire picture. When this diagonal intersects with other lines, tension is created. The diagonal need not be a literal line; it can be the arrangement of objects

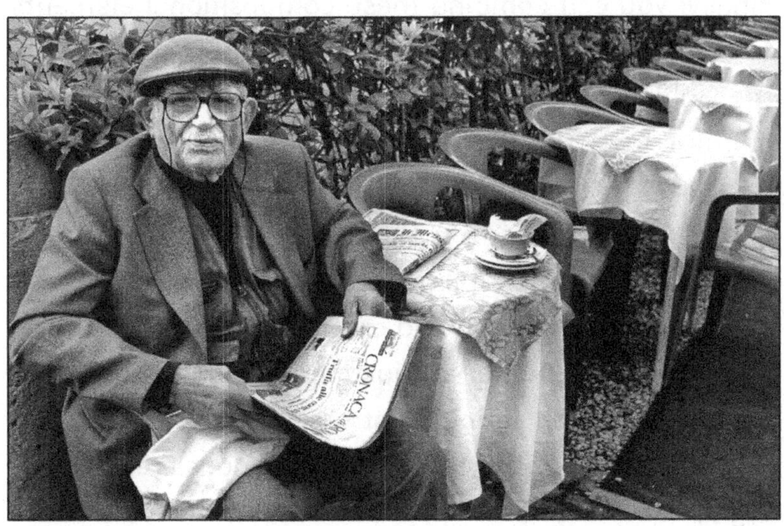

crossing the frame from one of the upper corners to the opposite lower corner. Returning to the concept of "choosing the right spot," consider this when you're shooting a diagonal composition. For example, you can take a portrait of four people straight on, or you can position yourself above (on a ladder, for instance) and tilt the camera so that your models align along a diagonal. In doing so, the picture will be more compelling.

It may not always be possible to arrange a diagonal composition that lines up from corner to corner. In geometry, any sloping line is considered a diagonal. The same goes for photography – any sloping line will provide a strong visual effect. The picture above was taken on a street in Milano, Italy. The setting is completely common and unspectacular, but the diagonal of the tables gives the visual an edge.

Finally, you can combine these compositional elements to create innumerable variations. For instance, combine the Golden Ratio with the diagonal by lining up a diagonal, not from the corners, but from the lower Golden Ratio to the upper one. Or combine the diagonal and symmetry by creating a symmetrical composition along a sloping line. The possibilities are endless; they only cease where your imagination and creativity does. These three composition elements are just the beginning, but they will grant you an infinitely stronger set of tools when composing your pictures. The world famous French photographer Henri Cartier-Bresson had his very own, beautiful definition of the perfect composition of a picture: „To take photographs means to recognize - simultaneously and within a fraction of a second - both the fact itself and the rigorous organization of visually perceived forms that give it meaning. It is putting one's head, one's eye and one's heart on the same axis."

3. Close-up on Emotions: Using Wide-angle Lenses

The famous war photographer, Robert Capa, once said, "If your pictures aren't good enough, you aren't close enough."

Long lenses may look impressive, but they should be relegated to the brand of photography for which they've been designed: in essence, classical portraits, sports, and nature shots. Long lenses capture beauty, wide lenses capture emotion and, as a photojournalist, emotion is what you're after. Your pictures will be more intense and striking if you get close to your subject with a wide lens.

A wide lens on your camera (below 50 mm) will actually force you into the action, and because of this, your picture will gain depth and emotional charge. Don't hesitate to get as close as a meter to your subject.

Unfortunately, this necessity of proximity when it comes to capturing emotion has cost many a photojournalist his/her life. A good illustration of this is Gerda Taro (the companion and professional partner of Robert Capa, quoted above), who was a war photographer in the early 1900s, and the first female photojournalist to cover the front lines. Taro died during her coverage of the Spanish Civil War. It's been said that Taro's shots were the only testament at the time to the reality at hand, as National-ist propaganda skewed this reality, claiming the Nation-alists had control over the region when, in fact, they'd been pushed out by the Republican forces. This goes to show just how important photojournalism can be: a pho-to can tell the truth in a world seething with lies.

James Nachtwey, a renowned American photojournalist, was the subject of a famous photograph illustrating the danger of the job. In the photo, he's crouched in the dirt, shooting pictures in the middle of a group of armed re-bels who are shooting to kill. This famous photo demon-strates the great lengths some photographers will go to in order to capture that perfect shot. In fact, more re-cently, Nachtwey was caught in the crossfire while on the job; shot in the leg during the Thailand political pro-tests of 2014. For most people, this willingness to die for a photograph – or for a story – is a heroism beyond com-prehension. But those brave photojournalists who have gotten close enough to the story to capture its truth serve the rest of us in doing so. They are humanity's col-lective microscope on the cellular makeup of the world.

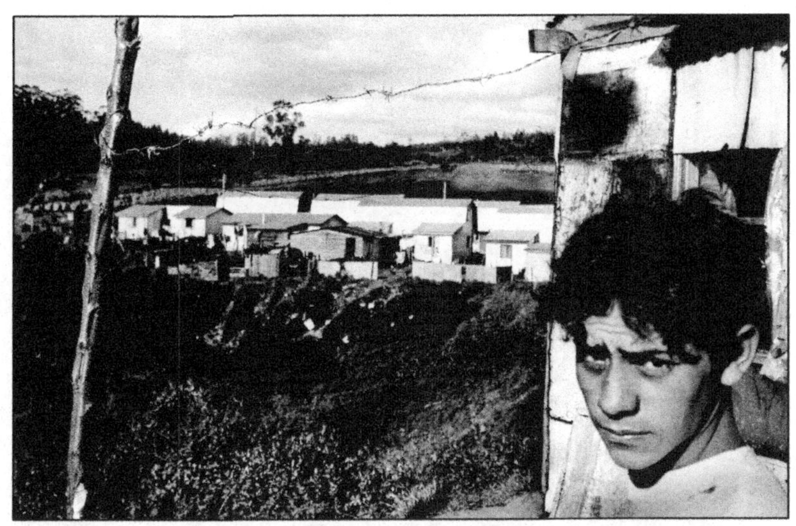

This picture was taken in a Chilean slum. The boy is the closest element in the photo. I took several pictures of him, but I don't think he realized that he was the focal point of this one. He stood on my right and, with the wide lens, I caught him in the corner with that furrowed brow. Though he is the focal point, the camera is focused on the barbwire, leaving the boy ever so slightly out of focus.

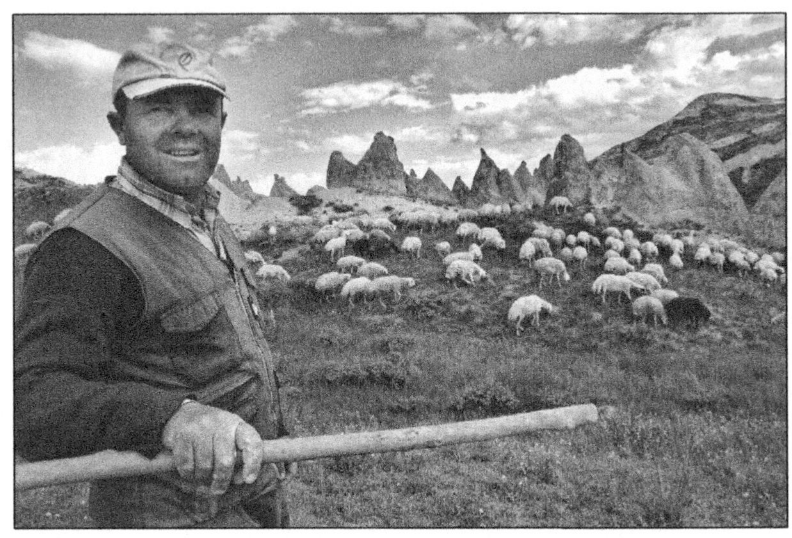

Taken in Cappadocia, a central region of Turkey, I spent a good amount of time with the shepherd in this photo. The wide-angle lens maintains a sharpness in all planes of the picture – from the hand to the face to the sheep and the mountains in the background. The slight distortion of perspective dramatizes the clouds' dynamics and pulls the viewer into the photo.

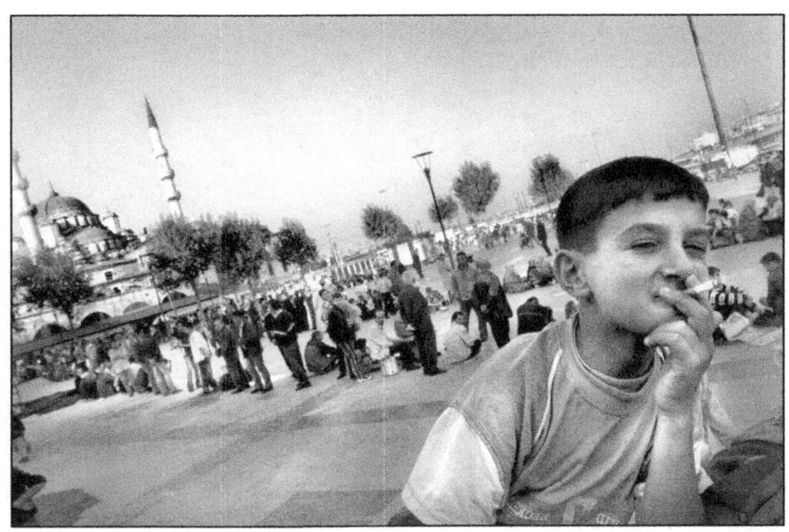

Shot in Istanbul, Turkey, again the wide-angle lens sharpens the entirety of the image, especially the boy, without taking away from the background, where the mosque is an important focal point. The apparent physical closeness of the boy is an impression brought on by the distortion.

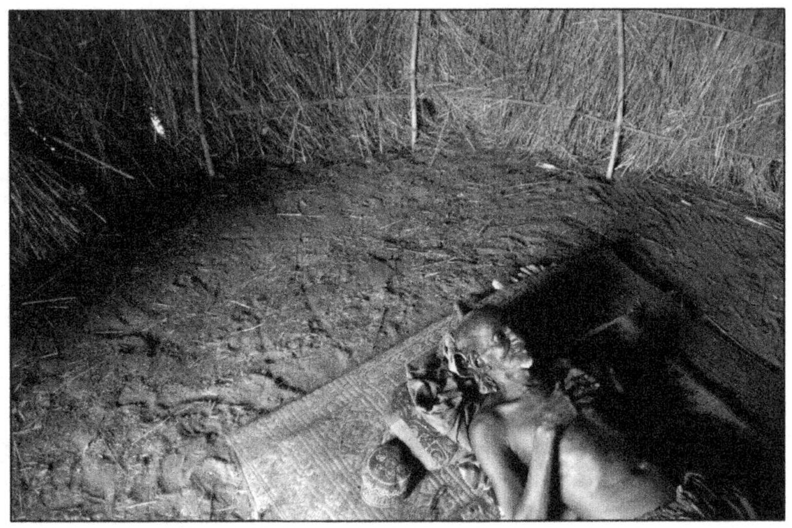

Without a wide-angle lens, this picture would have been impossible. There was simply not enough room in this old man's hut in northern Mali - although, with the lens, it looks like there's plenty. This is because wide-angle lenses distort space. Small spaces are stretched, an effect often used in publicity photography, particularly when it comes to commercial ads for hotel rooms.

4. A Picture is Worth A Thousand Words: Telling a Story with Your Lens

A good picture tells a story on its own. When your audience looks at your photographs, they should see the characters, the props, the plot; they should be able to interpret the story you're telling. Pictures are a form of communication, therefore to be a great photographer, you must be a great communicator and story-teller. You must compile all the elements of a story into your photo's composition. Sometimes the expression on a person's face is enough to tell a story – take, for example, Steve McCurry's famous *National Geographic* shot of the Afghani refugee. However, often you need an additional element in order to communicate the story. In fact, the McCurry photo was so captivating not only because of the young girl's intense gaze, but because the red shawl she wore complemented the otherworldly green of her eyes.

Apart from the elements that naturally exist, you may also choose to insert props into your photo. For example, if you're telling a story about an athlete's epic win, he or she might be holding the medal or trophy just won. Not only is the prop a literal plot element, but the model will concentrate on the held object and will be less disturbed by the camera if his or her hands are busy. A prop may be just what your model needs to feel more comfortable and relaxed, making him or her appear natural and authentic.

Background information is also vital to story-telling, therefore, choose your spot so that important elements either appear next to the model or are clearly visible in the background. Doing so will "set the scene," just as you would if you were a writer or director.

Sebastião Salgado is the undisputed master of story-telling photography. Take a look at his work. Every single shot tells a story. Among Salgado's enormous collections, he created "Genesis," a project that transported him all over the world and spanned seven years of his life, between 2004 and 2011. Genesis depicts untouched nature and indigenous communities, revealing humanity's roots in ancestral tradition, alongside nature's roots uncorrupted by man. This body of work collectively tells a story; however, each photo stands on its own, communicating its message. You need no text, no caption to understand the picture's essence and the narrative being told.

James Nachtwey once said: "For me, the strength of photography lies in its ability to evoke humanity. If war is an attempt to negate humanity, then photography can be perceived as the opposite of war."

In capturing war, horrific events, or hidden realities in a photograph, the photographer evokes the humanity in their audience by showing the audience itself in a mirror. As the audience, we feel empathy, we feel compassion, because we see ourselves in this darkness. This is the compelling nature of story-telling, and photojournalism is one of the strongest narrators; due to its visual nature, a photograph is tactile evidence of the reality at hand.

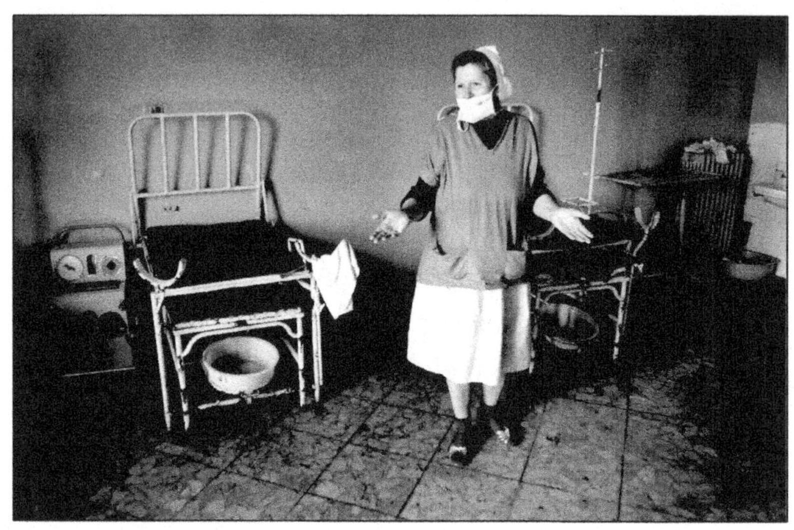

The nurse's body language tells a story of desperation and helplessness. Her "props" are the white hat and surgical mask, which indicate her profession – another element of the story. The background confirms that she is, indeed, involved in healthcare, and the equipment suggests that this is a delivery room. Considering the poor quality of the equipment and the unsanitary state of the room, you might easily guess the story's context: who would like to give birth to a baby in these conditions?

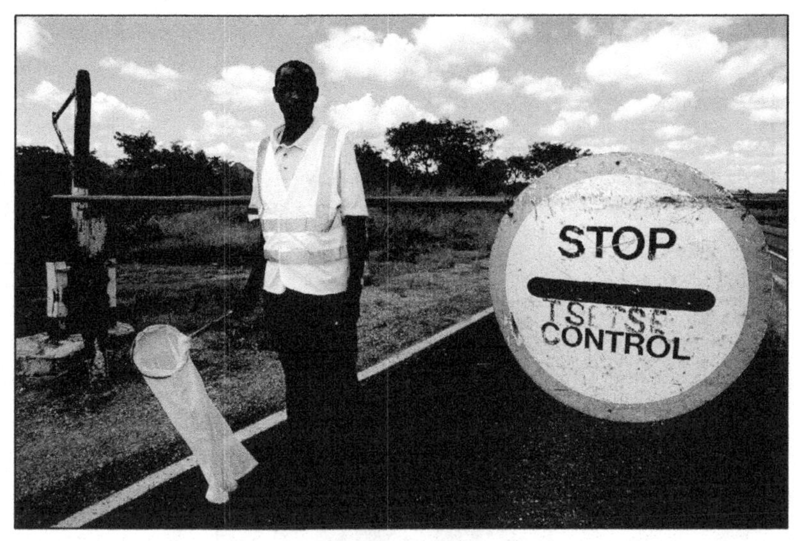

In the picture above, the wide-angle perspective and the dynamic sky evokes some strong visual impact, but the story is not easily told or understood. Shot in southern Tanzania, the man's uniform tells us that he is an official of some kind, while the stop sign confirms this authoritarian position. The stop sign also reads "Tsetse Control," and the man holds a net in his right hand. The man is actually in charge of controlling Tsetse flies, which are a dangerous disease-spreading insect. The official stops the cars in order to search inside for the dangerous flies, which he then catches and kills.

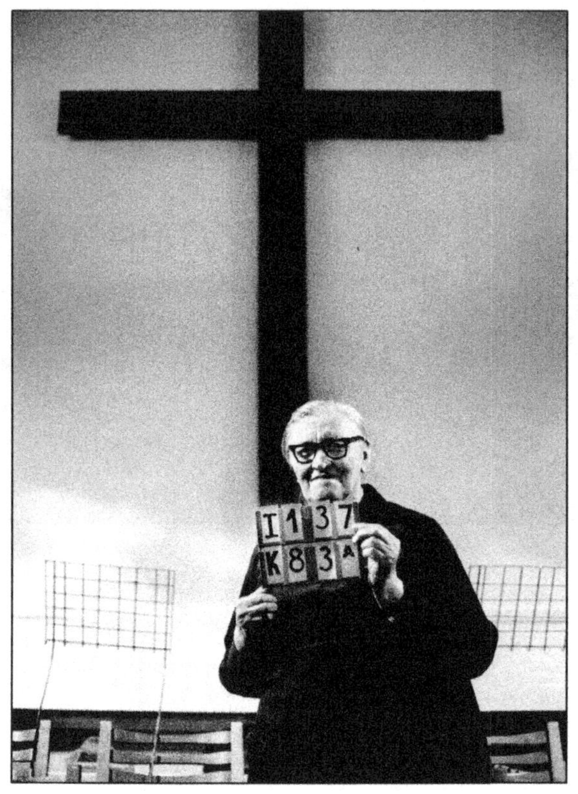

This picture was taken in Estonia during the country's struggle for independence from the Soviet Union. The partially captured cross centered in the background indicates that the setting is a church. The woman is presenting the page numbers to the congregation to lead them in song, essentially telling the story of Estonia's revolution, which was affectionately termed the "singing revolution."

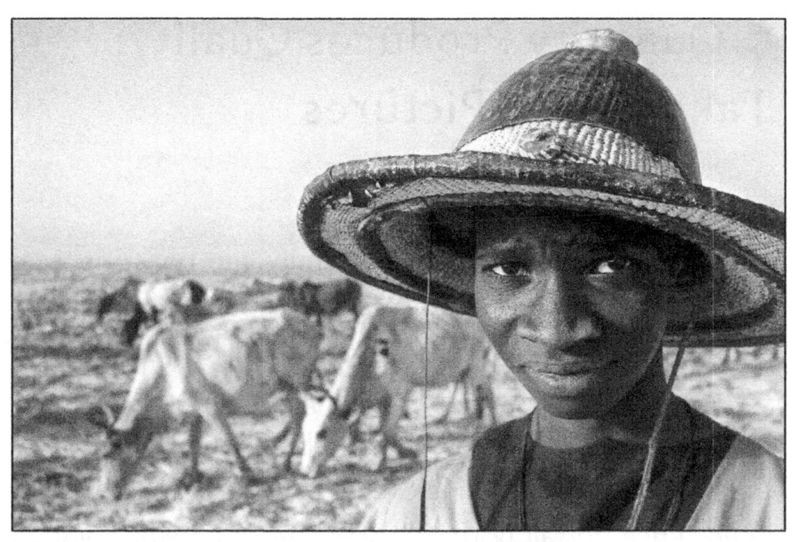

5. Quantity Produces Quality: Take Lots of Pictures

It's safe to assume that every family can boast at least one "perfect" family photo, a shot where all the right elements – light, models, composition, the moment – came together to tell a compelling story. Though it may have been a lucky shot, nevertheless, an excellent portrait resulted, and a single excellent portrait is all you need. Luck certainly does come into play when you're behind the camera as well; in fact, with a little luck, every Jane or John with a camera is capable of producing a powerful picture. But what distinguishes a "lucky" photographer from a good one, and a good photographer from a great one, is one's ability to consistently produce stellar pictures without the need for luck.

Although quality over quantity is a true earmark for the "best" of any profession, at least when you're a photographer just starting out, this is not necessarily the case. George Bernard Shaw once said, "A photographer is like a cod, which produces a million eggs in order that one may reach maturity." For beginners or for those photographers still shaping themselves, this is entirely true. In order to produce the "egg that reaches maturity," the simple trick is this: take lots of shots.

Years ago, when digital cameras were still a pipe-dream and photography equipment was so large it necessitated a crane for transport, taking lots of shots was expensive, laborious, and involved significant time in the lab. But, in the digital age, there is absolutely no reason not to shoot multiples to capture a single portrait. Doing so allows you to experiment with different shutter speeds, positions, lighting, etc. Elongating the shoot will also allow you to create a deeper – and, therefore, more authentic – relationship with your model, putting them at ease so that you might capture that moment of vulnerability that makes for a great photo: when your subject is most naturally and beautifully human. Annie Leibowitz once said that she needs three rolls for a portrait: one to get the model used to the situation, a second for the real work, and a third for backup.

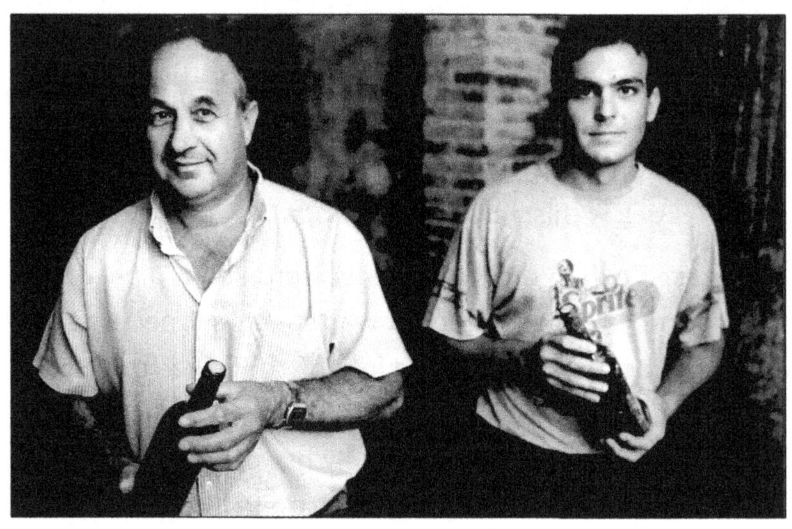

Men are often more difficult to photograph, because they are more likely to put up their guard around a camera. This particular shot was further complicated by a father/son relationship. Sometimes family portraits make the subjects even tenser, as the pre-existing relationship prevents them from willingly being vulnerable around each other. It took a couple of settings and lots of pictures, before I was able to catch these two in an expressive and natural way. Note, that the attractiveness of the picture is due a lot to the symmetry effect between father and son (see chapter 2).

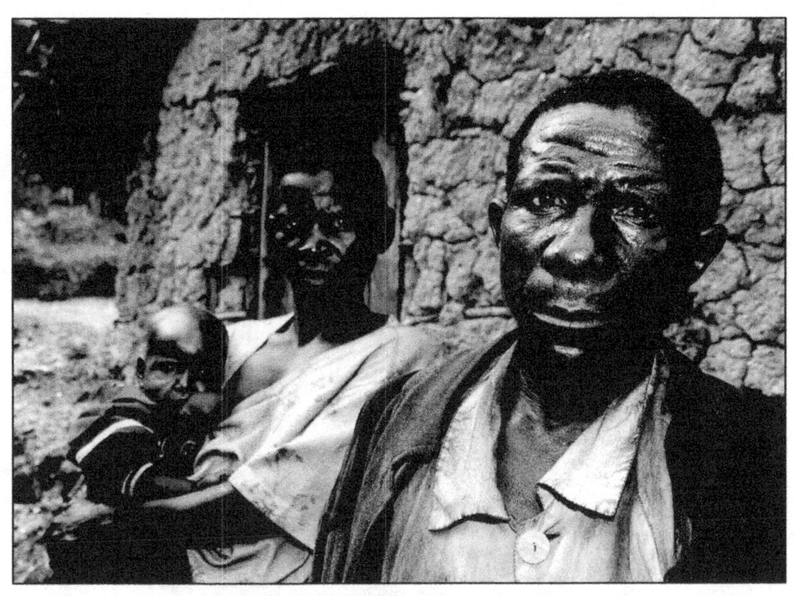

This is a selection of some discarded photos of the Burundi family, pictured above. These are four raw, unworked, uncut shots from about three dozen. Despite the serious expression on the man's face, as soon as the camera was lowered, we laughed and talked together.

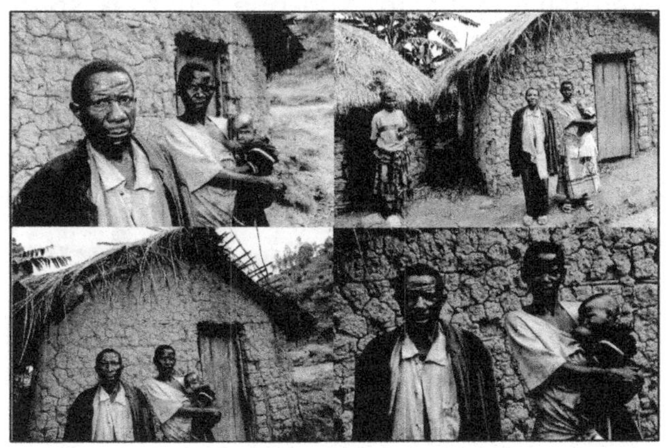

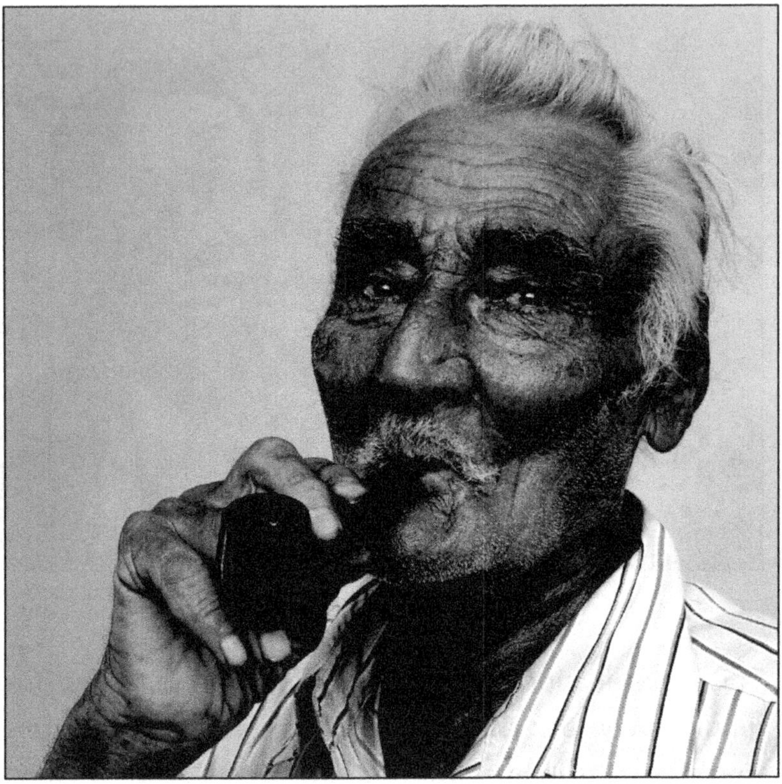

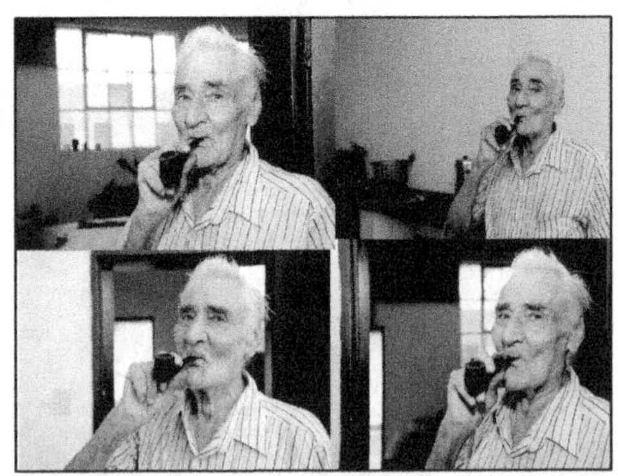

Again, this set of photos demonstrates how taking many shots can eventually result in "the one." It took some time to find the right angle and the right moment to capture this man's discreet and gentle smile.

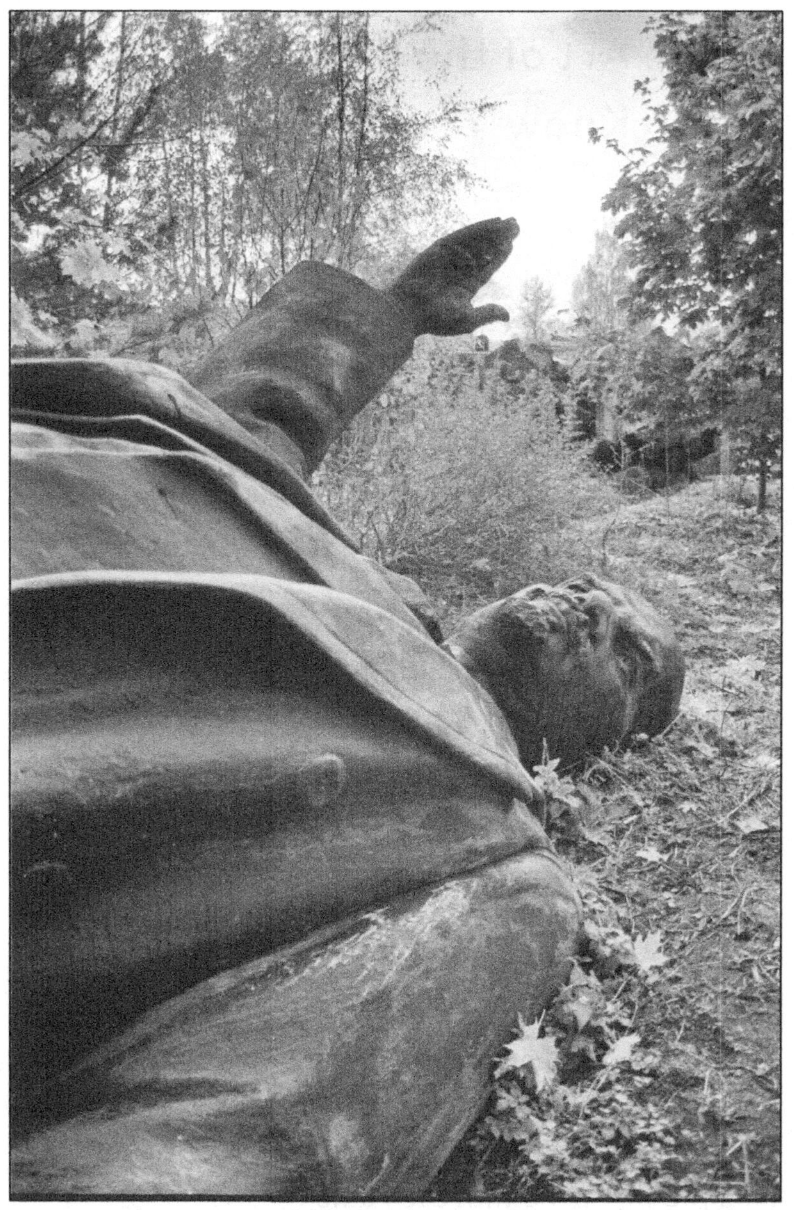

6. The Art of the Portrait: Get to Know Your Subject

Great portraiture distinguishes itself by distilling the essence of the subject's complex personality into a single photo. It is the sole responsibility of the photographer to conduct that distillation process. To do so, the photographer must pull the personality from the model and ensure that it's exhibited in the model's face, body, and attitude. One way to do this, of course, is to talk.

Talk with your subject while preparing a shot. Ask questions about the person's life, occupation, hobbies, passions, preferences, family, etc. Learn about the person and then tell their story through the photograph. Go on discussing while you arrange the light, while you put in your film and, finally, while you shoot. Photographing another person is an intimate act and can be frightening for the subject... and maybe even for you, as a beginning photographer. The best way to conquer that fear together is to build a true personal relationship in this brief time you will spend with each other.

Meeting many new and interesting people is one of the greatest pleasures of being a photographer, and so you must develop a brand of charisma or, at the very least, an appropriate bedside manner; in other words, you need to hone your interpersonal skills in order to quickly build trust with your subjects. One thing to keep in mind is that you, as the story-teller, should do more listening than talking. Don't lecture; have a dialogue that's more heavily weighted towards your subject. Ask questions, and show genuine interest through attentive listening and responding to your subject's answers.

Sebastião Salgado said it like this: "The picture is not made by the photographer. The picture is more good or less good in function of the relationship that you have with the people you photograph."

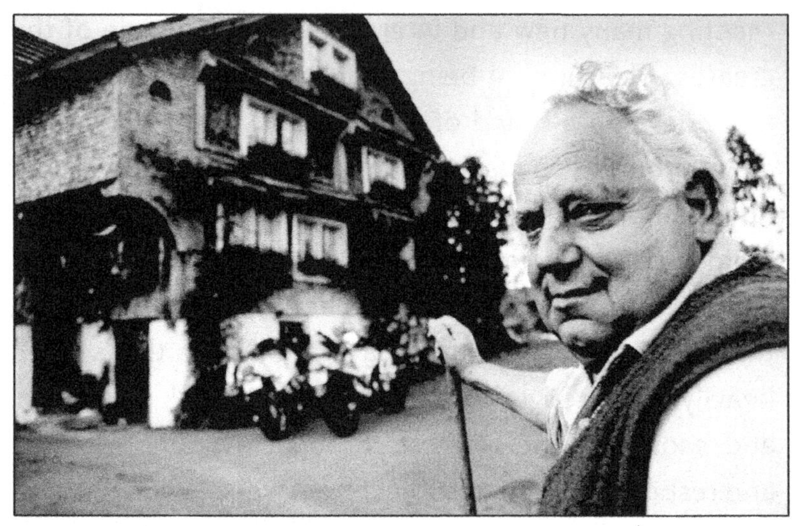

When shooting this incredibly camera-shy Swiss mountain man, this is the very last picture of the three rolls of film shot. In my brave attempt to uphold a conversation during the entire session, I often found myself coming up short. It was only when we walked back together toward the house (away from the original setting of the picture) that our relationship turned casual, and the man let his guard down. He turned to me to answer a question, and that is the moment of this picture.

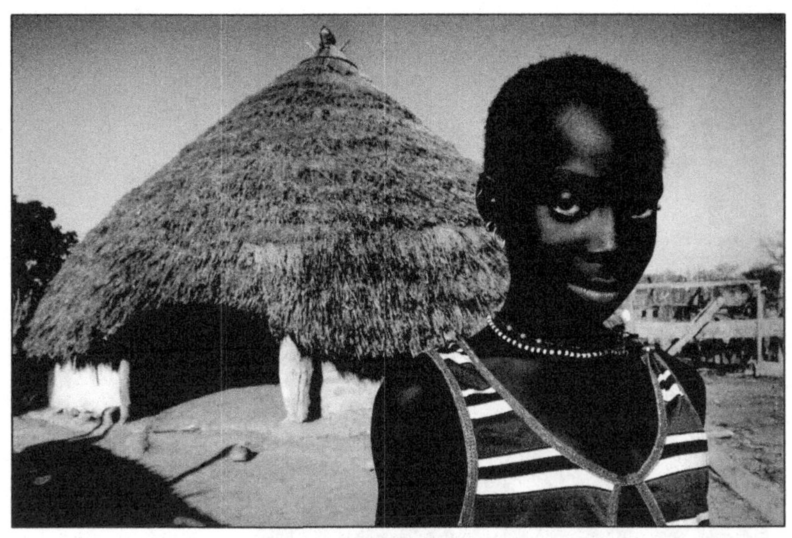

Children are often more natural and less camera-shy but, essentially, the same rules apply across the board when it comes to building that photographer-model relationship: show your interest. Be honest. Treat everyone with respect. Taking a picture is something intimate. If you use a wide-angle lens, you get very physically close to your subject, oftentimes trespassing in their "bubble," so to speak. People will only allow you to trespass if they trust you.

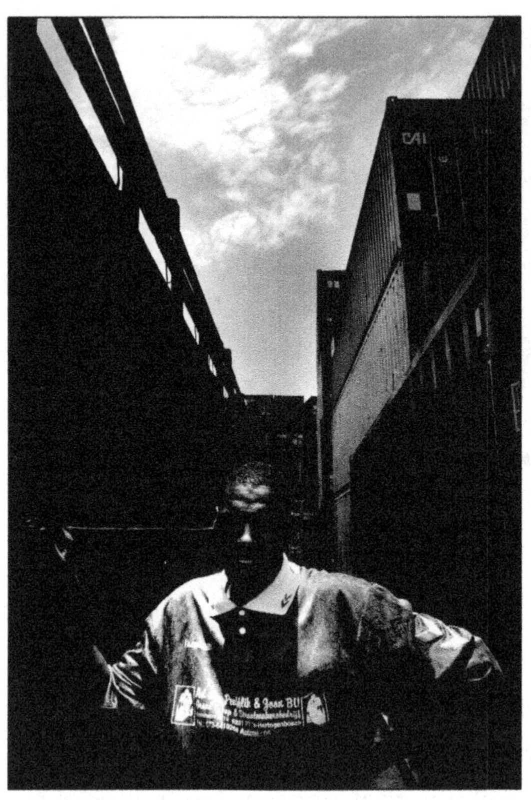

For standard portraits in the studio, the best lens is usually 85 mm to 105 mm. But as mentioned earlier, photojournalism is not about superficial beauty, but about emotions and story-telling, which holds a beauty of its own. A wide-angle is better suited for this task. All portraits in this chapter have been shot with a 50 mm lens or lower.

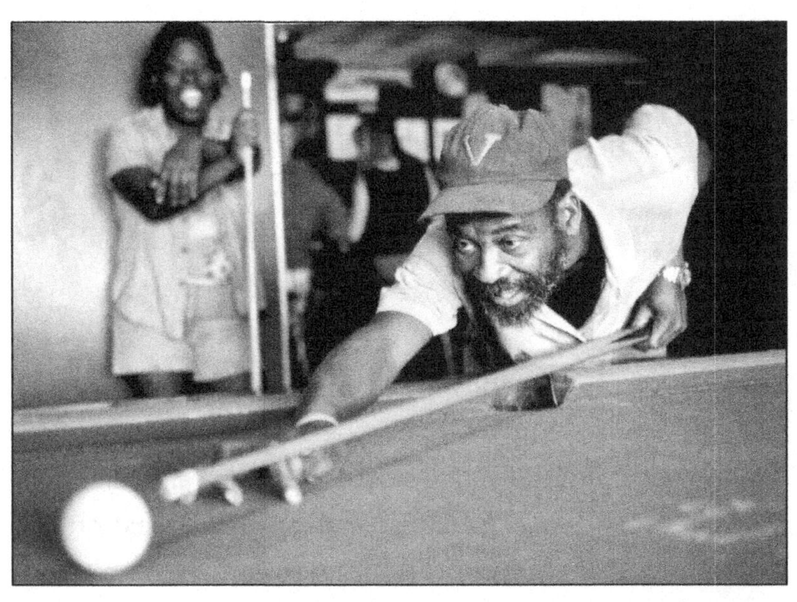

7. Pop! Pop!: Natural Light, Little Flash

Flash and photography have been together since the very beginning, but theirs can be a volatile relationship. If not used limitedly and with precision, artificial light can create artificial pictures, calling into question the authenticity of your photos. In order that you don't push the volatile relationship between flash and photography to that breaking point, start with the available natural light and use high-speed film rather than flash. Once you've assessed the natural light available to you, you'll be able to better target specific areas of the picture that require flash.

You should also avoid mounting the flash on the camera. Doing so is convenient, but gives off a fairly unnatural frontal light. Instead, carry a flash cord of 3 meters and either hold the flash in one hand as far away from the camera as possible, so that the angle on the subject's face is not frontal, or place the flash on a small tripod and direct the light to whatever needs lighting; the background behind a subject, for instance.

You may also use the flash indirectly, against a wall, a piece of paper, or a special reflector mounted on the flash. This is easy and straightforward in black-and-white photography, but be careful when you attempt this with colored photos. Reflections from colored surfaces may change the hue of your picture.

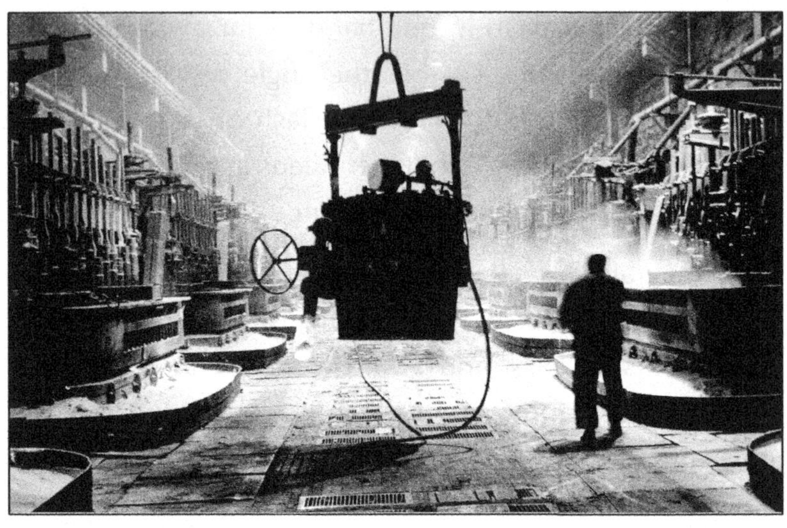

The picture above was taken in an aluminum factory in Slovakia in the early nineties. The huge magnetic field of the electrically powered machines wreaked havoc on my camera. I took all the batteries out and worked in manual mode, thereby having no other option than to use the available light. But doing so was to my advantage; the natural light just happened to accentuate the depth of the room, while providing the photo with visual dramatization, as well as a touch of reality.

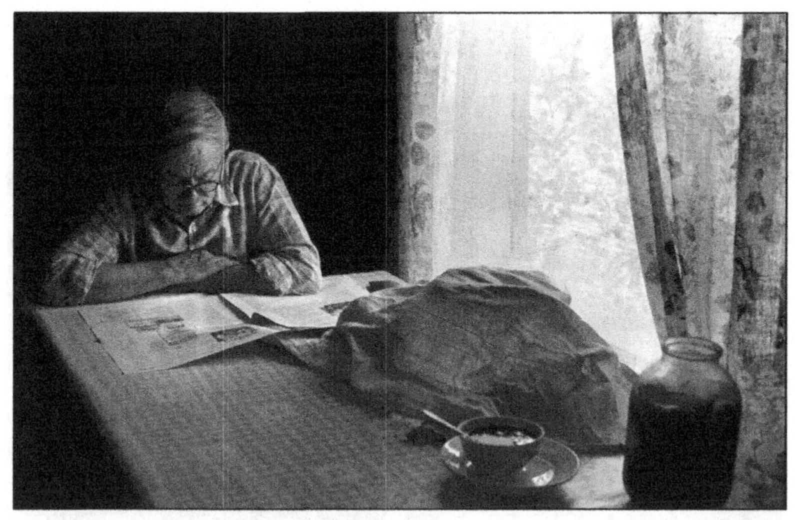

No flash was used in this picture. The only light source was the natural light coming through the window. The old Abkhazian man was reading a newspaper in the morning after his breakfast. A couple months after this picture was taken, he was forced to flee his home and his kitchen table due to civil war.

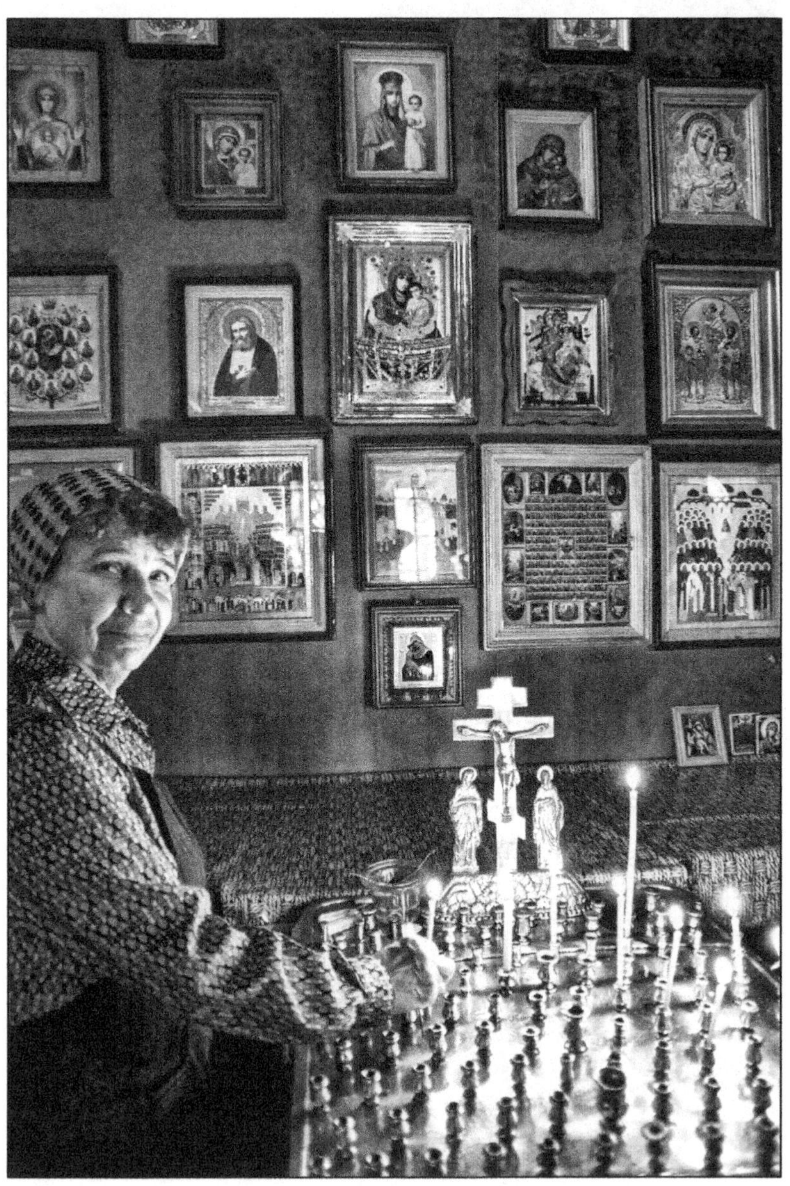

8. Post-Production: Working Your Prints

When using film, work in the dark room is essential for the quality of your picture. The dark room is where you turn good pictures into perfect ones. Today, of course, your digital "dark room" is the computer screen. A few standard tricks are outlined below. These tips are primarily for black-and-whites, but are also applicable to color.

Darken the sky. A darker sky dramatizes the photo's story. If you darken all four corners, you create an effect which is called a "vignette." This provides portraits with an "old touch" but is usually detested by editors.

Lighten the whites of the eyes and teeth. The contrast will dramatize the portrait's expressiveness and will draw the viewers' attention to the most essential feature of a portrait: the eyes.

Darken any nonessential parts of the picture. Again, the viewer's attention is drawn toward the light, so you are literally highlighting the important parts of the story for your viewers and, in contrast, subduing the nonessentials. Doing so will direct the absorption of the story.

And finally crop, crop and crop! Always crop the picture a little more than your gut instinct may instruct. The more you crop away, the more pronounced the picture's visual effect will be. Don't hesitate to cut the top of the head or limbs if doing so doesn't eliminate a vital prop. This will expand the size of the eyes and draw the subject closer to the spectator.

Please note that editing is particularly subjective. Not all editors like tight cropping. Some prefer space around the subject in the original, so that they may have room to crop the picture themselves.

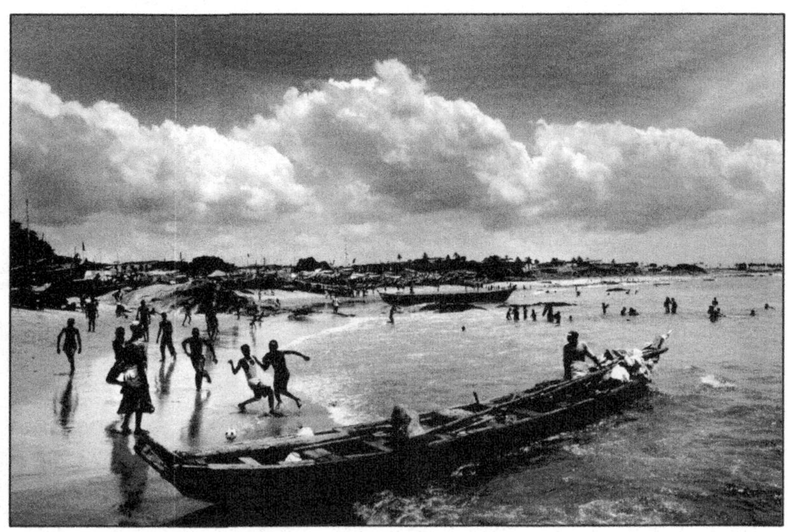

This picture experienced some quite heavy post production. The sky was darkened and contrasted. The area in which the kids are playing was highlighted to heighten the impact of the reflections and to attract attention to this important part of the picture. The kids and the boat were also sharpened slightly. As you can imagine, sharpening was a tool unavailable in the old dark rooms, but in the digital format, it can be an important tool when telling your story.

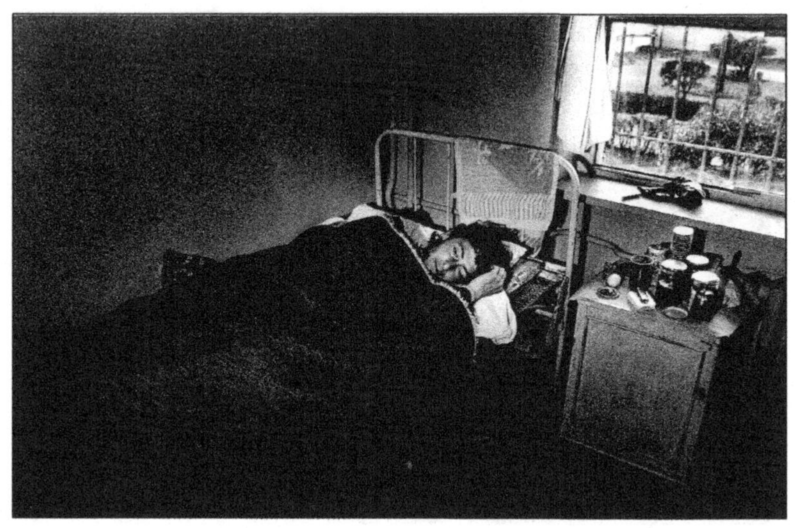

This picture was shot in Albania in the early nineties. In post-production, the window, curtain, pillow, drugs, and face have been lit, while the wall, covers, and floor have been heavily darkened. The original shot is on the right. Without the post-production changes, the photo is flat and unimpressive.

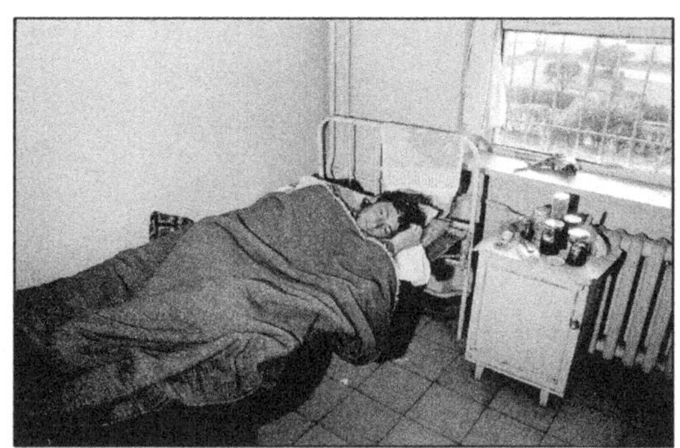

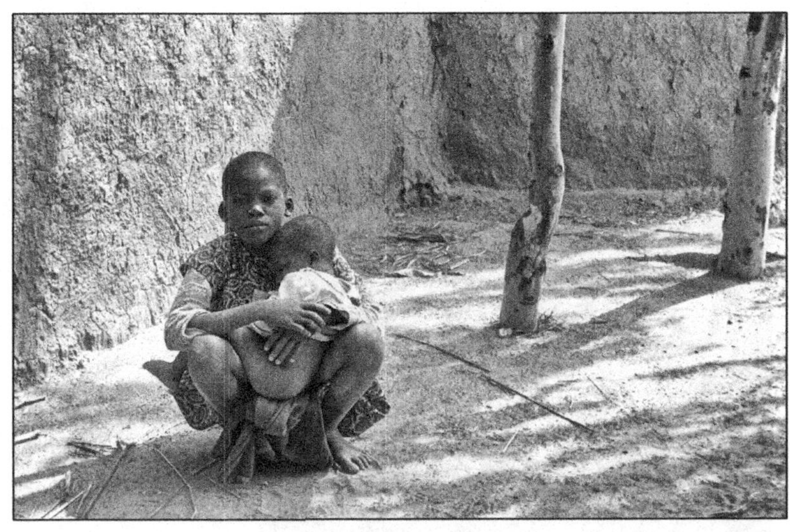

Digital print has also brought about some important and even ethical issues: as photographers and editors, how far are we allowed to go in enhancing a photo? If you intend for the picture to be published, then any alteration may be critical. When you digitally edit your photo, do so limitedly. In fact, it would be wise only to edit as far as was possible in the old-fashioned dark room (i.e. darken, lighten, contrast, and alter color tones). Any retouching should be strictly limited to cleaning the picture of spots due to dirt on the sensor or lens. The above example is an original of a girl sitting in front of a small tree, holding her sibling. It was edited limitedly, only in order to make the two children stand out.

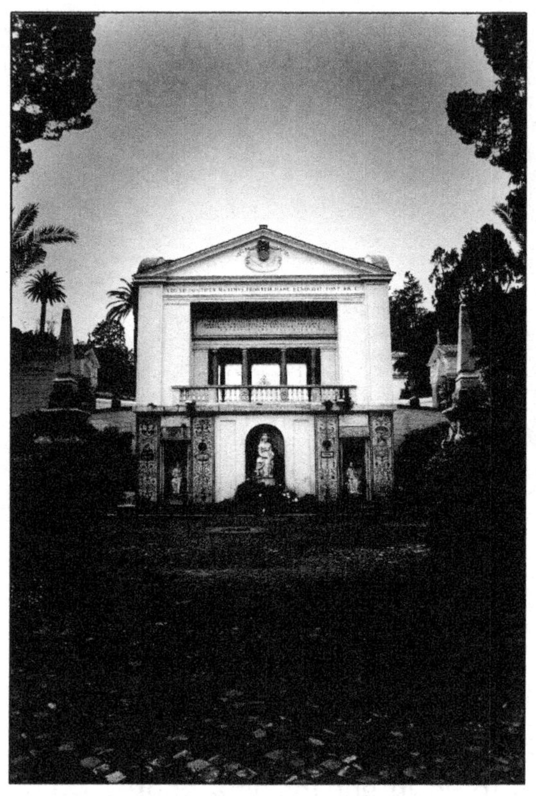

This is an example of a perfectly boring picture, if left untouched; however, with the darkening of the sky and the contrast of the building, you create a passable illustration of the Vatican garden.

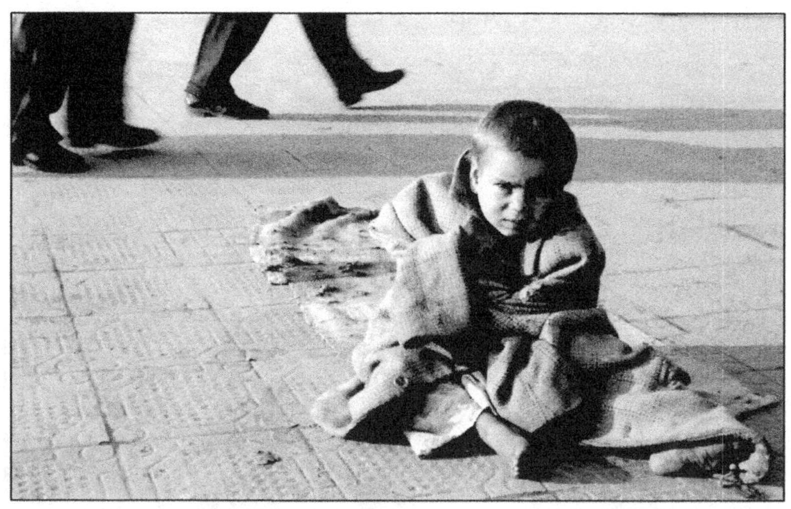

This picture tells a story about the clash of social classes. In the background, men in shiny shoes pass by a starving, begging child. If you see the full-frame, the photo is less effective, because the men are actually not attired like the elite and the surroundings are rather blase, but cropping to a tighter frame emphasizes the message.

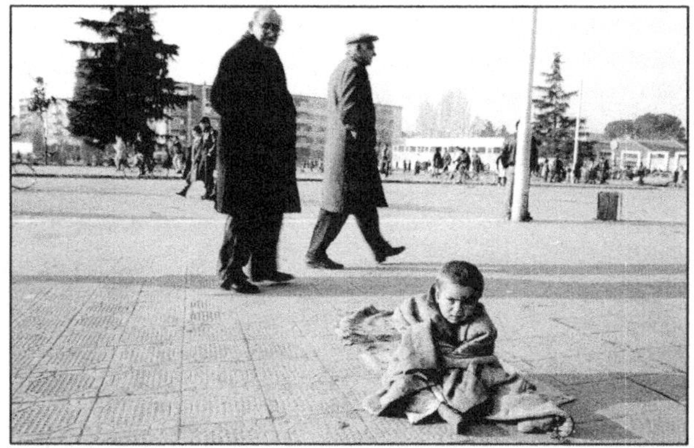

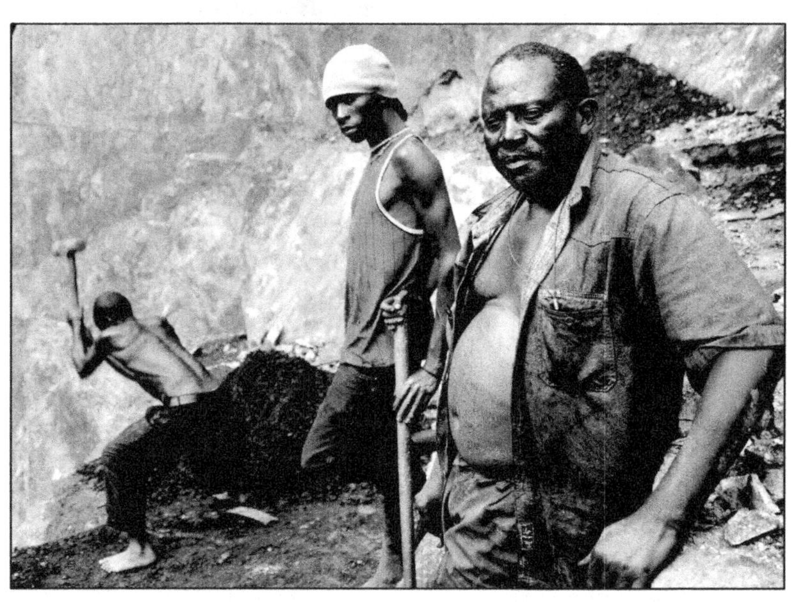

9. The Cutting Room Floor: Be Selective

If you follow chapter 5's advice, you'll end up with a lot of material, so much so that you might not know what to do with it. But once you've arrived at post-production, you've reached the cutting room floor...so now's the time to cut. Be very selective with the pictures you retain. Settle on one picture per subject. Always keep only the best one, and put the others out of your head. This is sometimes difficult to do, but self-restraint is key to maintaining your ideal collection.

So how do you settle on just a single photograph? One photo may have the better light, while the other has more compelling emotion. After a while, they may even all start to look exactly the same. The question to ask yourself is: when it comes to the perfect shot, which quality trumps all? For yourself, perhaps emotion is the key indicator of perfection; for another photographer, the composition may trump emotion. Showing multiple photos of the same shot is not an option, as doing so will only attract attention to their respective weaknesses and will steal the soul from your photography.

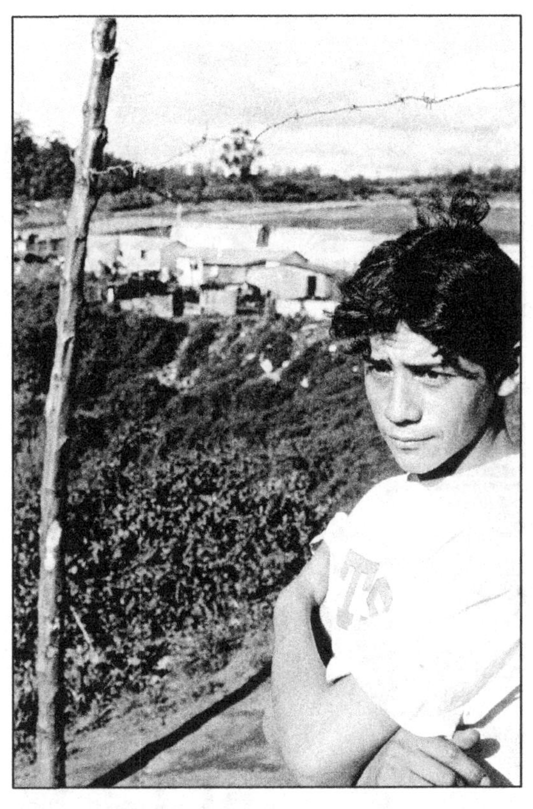

This is the same setting as the photo in chapter 3, but there's one difference: the boy is sharp, while the barb-wire is slightly unfocused. Technically speaking, this is probably the better picture. But my preference lies with the first picture, due to the expression on the boy's face. Therefore, I chose to discard this one and, aside from training purposes, no one will ever see it.

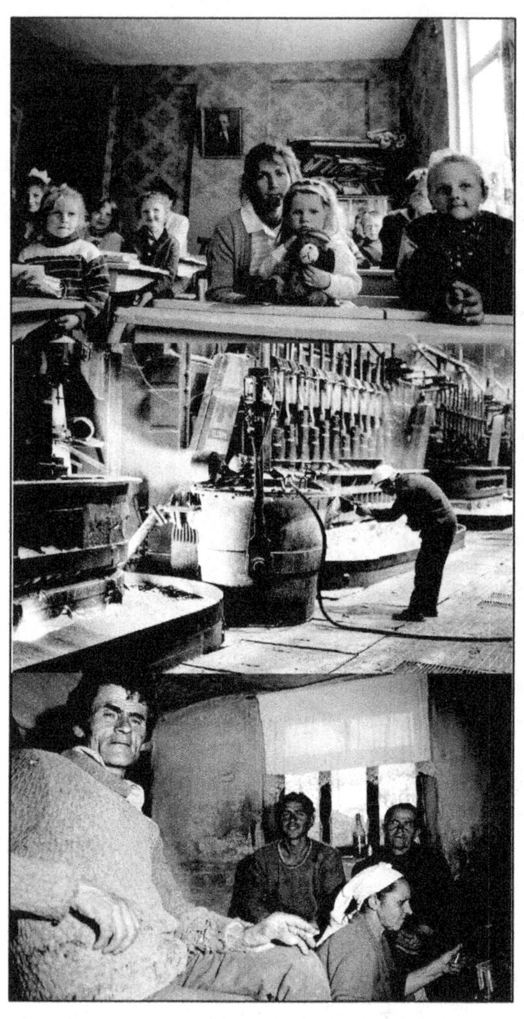

This is a selection of discarded and unworked photos to contrast with those previously used in this book. As you can see, they each have their merits, and some viewers may prefer these over the shots I, myself, chose. This just goes to show that personal preference comes highly into play in the cutting room. Often selection is one of the most difficult tasks.

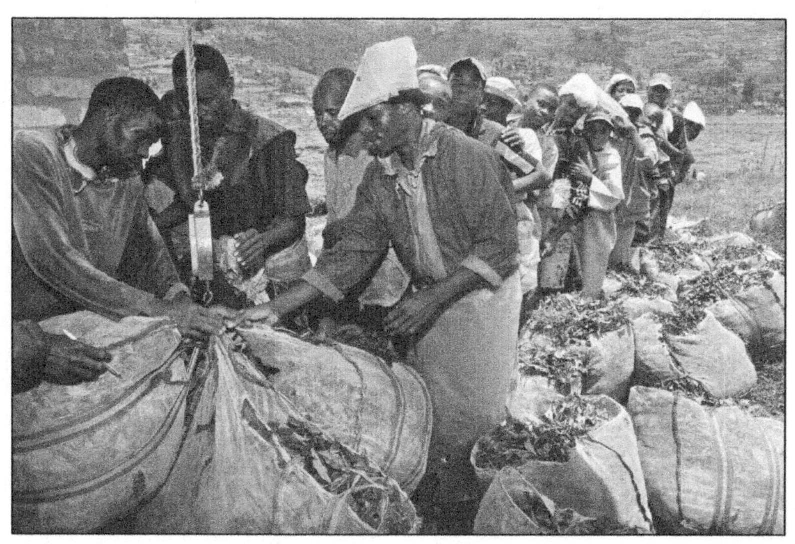

10. Narcissus:
Put a Human in the Picture

A final remark. So far we have not specifically discussed the subject of your photos. Well, that's because, when it comes to photojournalism, the answer is simple: a picture is never as compelling without a person in it.

To demonstrate this, I recommend that you flip through your nearest magazine or newspaper and count the pictures sans people. I think you'll find that people-less pictures are very, very rare. Even when a building is the focal point of a photo, the journalist will wait for a person to enter or seek out some other possibility to include a person in the frame. The reason for this is also simple: we humans are narcissists. We like to see ourselves in print. Not necessarily our literal selves, but most definitely other humans. As previously stated, the photographer evokes the humanity in their audience by showing the audience itself in a mirror. As the audience, we are much more likely to be attracted to a photo if we see our own reflection, so to speak. No matter how humble an individual is, humanity, as a whole, is largely vain as Narcissus. To feel connected to a photo, we must see other humans in it, in order to compare and contrast our own human experience with the story that's being told.

There is a simple hierarchy of attractiveness when it comes to inclusion of objects in a photo, and the hierarchy ranks as follows:

1) People

2) Animals

3) Inert objects

So whatever job you've received as a photojournalist, take care to include a person in the picture. This small and simple step will greatly improve your chances of publication.

Though neither of the pictures on the next page is a very good one, they illustrate the topic under review. The picture below was taken a couple of seconds prior to the picture above. Though the railing frames the ship nicely in the photo below, it is without life and can't compete with the one above, despite the fact that the people in the latter photo are relegated to the shadows.

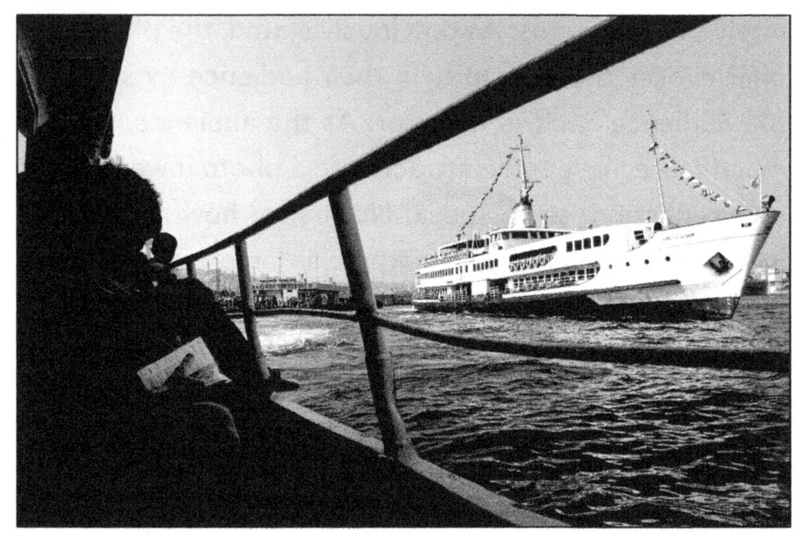

A good picture shows humans. In the words of Sebastião Salgado: „It's not the photographer who makes the picture, but the person being photographed."

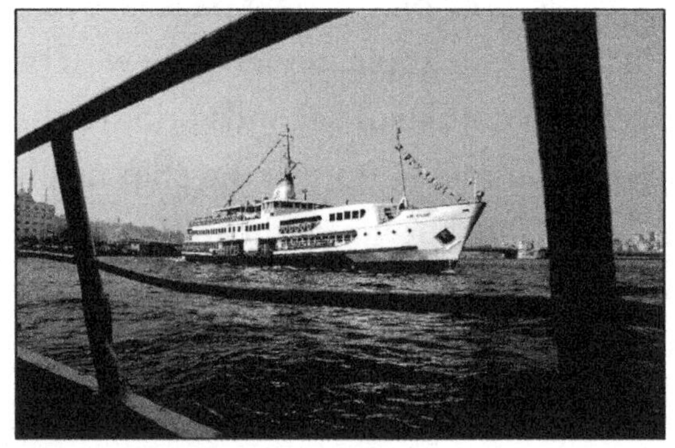

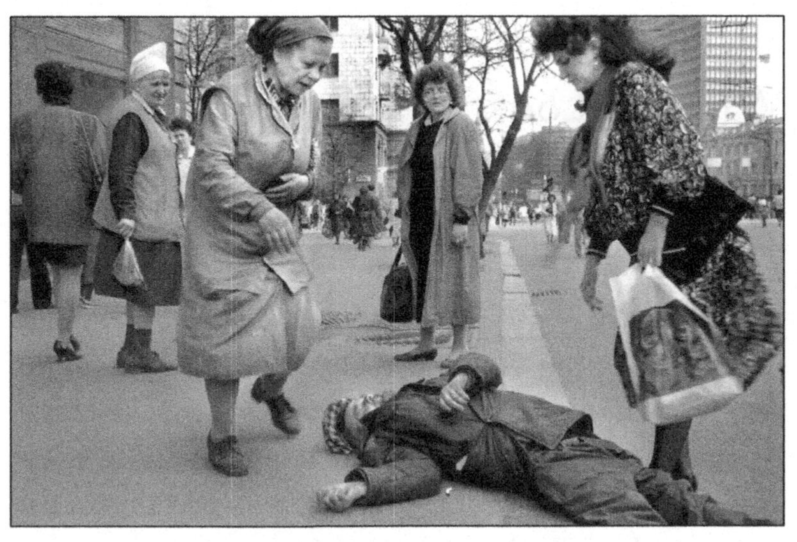

11. Your Story-Telling Tool: What to Look for in a Camera

A professional photojournalist would be nothing without a camera. As the essential tool for story-telling, you'll only want the best, and only a couple of brands seriously compete for this market. Being that a professional camera will run you at least a couple grand, you'll probably want to do your homework before you buy, unless you've got that kind of change jingling around in your pockets. Photography magazines are the best source of information when it comes to comparing the technical details of the latest models; but here are four general tips for starting out and buying your first professional camera.

1. Whatever camera you have on-hand is a good starter camera

You do not necessarily need a professional camera to make professional pictures. Today's top-line amateur cameras produce high-quality pictures, more than sufficient for publication in most newspapers and magazines. I actually started my career with a low-cost Minolta, and only later switched to my preferred brand, Nikon.

2. If you're not rolling in the dough, spend what little you have on lenses

In the old days, a good camera retained its value for years on end. In the digital world, chips become faster and better every year, and a camera loses its value at lightning speed. My old, mechanical Nikon F3, issued somewhere in the late 80s, is far more valuable than the digital Nikon D2H I bought in 2004. On the other hand, a good optical lens will remain a good optical lens. I still use my old manual lenses on my new Nikon cameras. So, a word of advice: if you are short on money, hold off on purchasing an expensive camera and buy a good lens instead. Taking quality pictures now with proper lenses will improve your potential for publication, enabling you to purchase your dream camera at a later date...when it will likely be replaced by a "better, newer, faster" camera anyway.

3. Choose a system, not a camera

A good lens only retains its value, if you can mount it on future generations of cameras. Therefore, you should choose a system, not a camera. Good brands will ensure compatibility of lenses, flashes, and cameras over multiple generations. To be honest, for serious photojournalism, only two brands stand the test of time: Nikon or Canon. I chose Nikon in the late 80s, and today I still use some of the equipment I bought then.

4. Choose the camera you like

All pro-cameras are going to be the best of the best. The only difference is a difference of opinion. So choose a known brand, and then let your gut decide. When you're test-driving, take the camera in your hand. If you like the feel, the balance, and the fit in your palm, then buy it. You will have to work with this tool every day, so don't be swayed by the technicalities; buy based on your own personal intuition.

And finally, when choosing your camera, think of the words of photographer Jessica Lange: "The camera is an instrument that teaches people how to see without a camera."

12. Quality: Why a "Pro" Camera Matters

So if you can take a "professional" shot without a professional camera, then why purchase that thousand dollar pro-camera anyway? What are the main reasons to fork over the cash, if essentially you're turning out the same quality as you would with a top-line amateur model? Well, there are a number of reasons to invest in your profession, some of which are outlined below.

Reliability

If your intention is to be a photojournalist or photographer, then your camera will be used every day. With a pro-camera, the shutter will retain precision even after a hundred thousand shots. Being that expensive and sturdy material, such as magnesium alloy or carbon, is used in the camera's construction, pro-cameras will also remain intact if banged around a bit. These materials absorb shock better than those in a cheap camera. I once dropped my Nikon F3 hard on a marble floor in Helsinki. The thing is virtually indestructible; it went on working without a hitch. The "indestructible" quality of pro-cameras is essential for photojournalism, as your job might place you in dangerous situations or highly destructible conditions, where the odds of coddling your camera are highly unlikely. The most important feature of a pro-camera is simple: it always, always works.

Quality

Often, pro-cameras have the newest chips and the best software. In standard settings and conditions, you won't notice the difference, but as soon as you are in a low-light setting, the superior quality of a pro-camera will be obvious. With a good pro-camera, the potential for the conditions of your prospective environments can expand. You will be able to take superior pictures in a far broader variety of spaces than with an amateur camera.

Speed

Pro-cameras are fast. If you want to do more than land-scape photography, you will need the speed. There is virtually no delay between the release and the photo snap. A pro-camera can often shoot up to eight pictures per second, and when you want to look at a picture on the monitor, it appears immediately, without any time-lapse.

Special functions

And finally, pro-cameras offer many special functions. Being that professional photographers often advise in the development of pro-cameras, new and improved functions are applied to each new model. Some of them come in very handy (like programmable function buttons) and some are seldom used (like the ability to close the viewer or lift the mirror manually - both for long exposures). For instance, a function on the old F3 allowed for operability without any battery (i.e. purely mechanical). I used this function in a coal mine in Albania, a photo of which appears in on the next page. For safety reasons, I was not permitted to take any electrical equipment into the mine. Any spark can potentially be lethal.

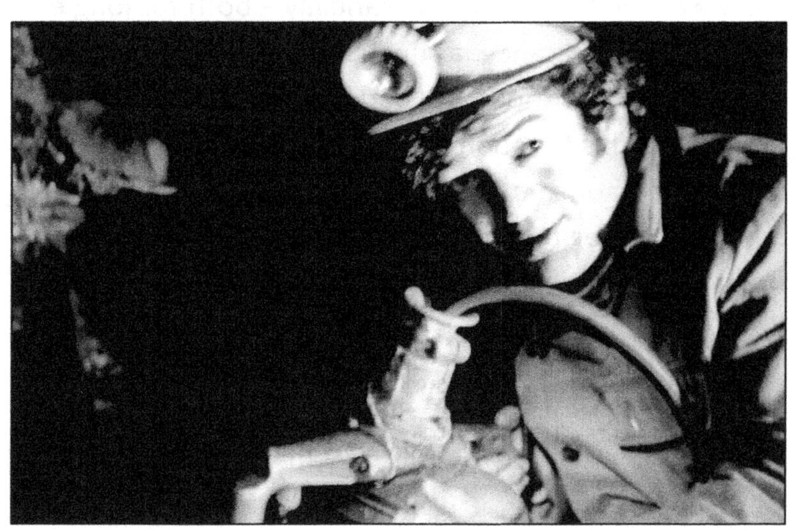

13. No Newbie:
How to Look Like a Pro

A photojournalist will immediately recognize a pro-colleague. If you're new on the job or if you're an engaged amateur, then these tips will enable you to feign some experience and, thereby, earn some respect. Although you shouldn't take your greenness too seriously, you probably don't want to be looked at like a newbie on the job. However, it's important to note that, in the long run, your only street cred will be your work.

- Don't walk around with a long tele on your camera. If you've read chapter 3, then you'll know why. The "always ready" lens for most journalists will be a wide-angle to lower-tele zoom (for instance 28 mm to 80 mm...that is, if zooms are used at all).

- Never – I repeat, never – try and show off a long and thin lens. Real professionals need lenses with high luminosity (better than 1:2). These lenses are wide. Rule of thumb: the wider the lens, the more light the chip receives, and the more flexibility you'll have to take a picture. Second rule of thumb: the wider the lens, the more expensive the lens.

- Don't let your camera hang around your neck. If you are working daily, you will quickly move your tool to your shoulder. Before the digital era, professionals walked around with two or three cameras hanging on them like bulbs on a Christmas tree. In those days, every camera had its spot: left shoulder, right shoulder, and the neck. Today, one camera is enough, and its rightful place is on your shoulder.

- Don't show off your big new camera bag. A camera bag should be light, as small as possible, very resistant and, last but not least, it should look old and used. Going digital has reduced the need to haul around a ton of equipment, and many of my colleagues own no camera bag at all; they simply place their tool in a normal bag hanging from the shoulder. It's less showy, but a lot more convenient when you're carrying it around the entire day.

- Don't worry about scuffs and scratches. Keeping your camera too clean, shiny, and show-ready may indicate that you care more about it than the story. The biggest difference between a pro-camera and a top-notch amateur camera is not the function, nor is it the quality of the pictures. The difference is the sturdiness, reliability, and resistance of the material. When you're under pressure and navigating imperfect conditions, you need a tool that can survive an accidental bang against a wall (my sympathy is with the wall, if it's an old Nikon F3; you can't destroy this camera).

- Finally, if you want to look like a pro, then you have to know your material, it has to exist in your heart. You need to be able to handle your camera in a every situation, whether that's at night, when you're awoken from a deep sleep by a story, or under high pressure, in the case of time-crunch or as a result of the desperate conditions in which you're shooting. In fact, you're professionalism and self-assurance in the handling of your working tool will also give the subjects you're shooting confidence and trust in you.

Please note that by following these rules, you're highly unlikely to fly under the radar: you'll still be recognized immediately as the new kid on the block. Photojournalists often know each other, at least if they work in the same city. Don't forget rule number 1: in the case of an event worth shooting, they'll likely be jockeying for the same spot as you. Show you're game by beating them to the punch!

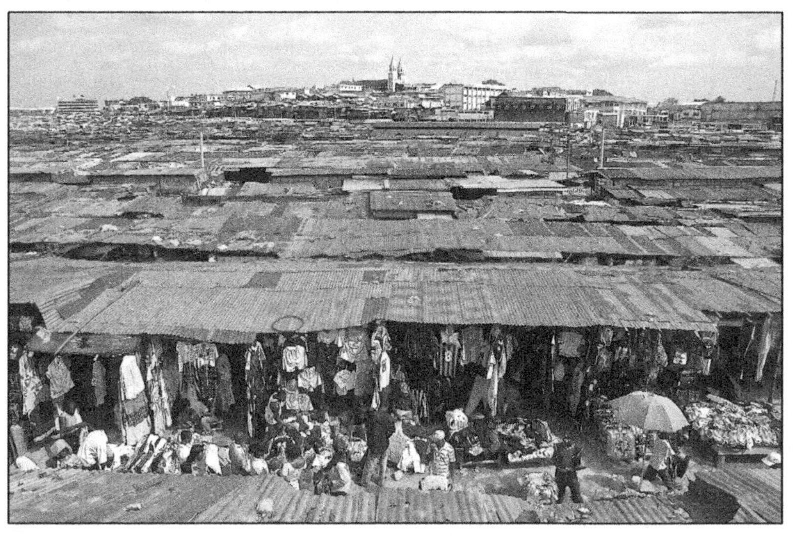

Acknowledgment

I would like to thank Christian Würtenberg. Without him, the pictures in this book might not exist. He introduced me to photography. He helped me discover Eastern and Central Europe during the tumultuous years of a falling Iron Curtain. His fearlessness was a glaring example for me as to the power of investigative journalism. Christian was murdered in 1992 during the Yugoslavian war while researching a story.

Captions

Title: Tobacco Farm (Moçambique), 2010

Page 6: Tea farmer, Buganda (Uganda), 2010

Page 8: Djemaa El-Fna, Marrakech (Morocco), 2004

Page 12: School in Abkhazia (Republic of Georgia), 1992

Page 13: Albanian mountains (Albania), 1991

Page 14: St. Gallen (Switzerland), 1992

Page 15: Worker, Aluminum Factory, (Slovakia), 1990

Page 18: Tobacco carrying child (Mozambique), 2010

Page 20: Leonardsville (Namibia), 2010

Page 21: Milano, (Italy), 2007

Page 25: Slum in Valdivia (Chile), 1996

Page 26: Shepherd, Capadoccia (Turkey), 2008

Page 27: Istanbul (Turkey), 2006

Page 28: Fulani tribe (Mali), 2008

Page 32: Women's hospital, Tirana (Albania), 1991

Page 33: Tse-tse control, Shingela (Zambia), 2010

Page 34: Church in Tallinn (Estonia), 1990

Page 35: Shepherd in Mopti (Mali), 2008

Page 38: Winegrower, Rioja Region (Spain), 1998

Page 39: Farmer in Ngozi (Burundi), 2010

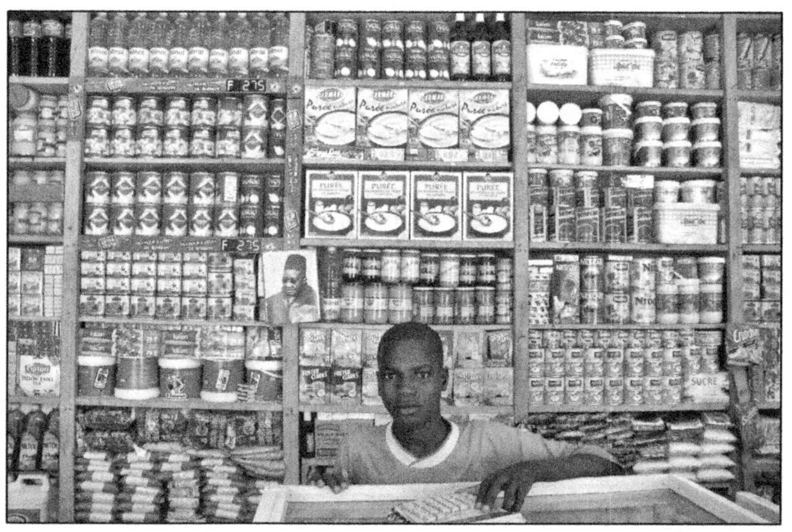

Made in United States
North Haven, CT
08 December 2023

45363719R00049